ON TWO SHORES

First published in 2006 by
The Dedalus Press
13 Moyclare Road
Baldoyle
Dublin 13
Ireland

www.dedaluspress.com

ISBN 1 904556 49 3

Dedalus Press titles are represented and distributed in the USA and Canada
by Dufour Editions Ltd., PO Box 7, Chester Springs, Pennsylvania 19425,
and in the UK by Central Books, 99 Wallis Road, London E9 5LN.

Printed and bound in the UK by Lightning Source, 6 Precedent Drive,
Rooksley, Milton Keynes MK13 8PR, UK.

Special thanks are due to Junko Ohno for all her help in preparing the
Japanese texts for this book.

The Dedalus Press gratefully acknowledges the
sponsorship of Aichi Shukutoku University, Japan,
in the production of this book.

The Dedalus Press receives financial assistance from
An Chomhairle Ealaíon / The Arts Council, Ireland.

ON TWO SHORES
New and Selected Poems

Mutsuo Takahashi

Translated from the Japanese by
Mitsuko Ohno & Frank Sewell

ACKNOWLEDGEMENTS

The author and translators wish to thank the following people for their support and encouragement:

Jean Bleakney, Scott Boltwood, David Burleigh, Ciaran Carson, Theo Dorgan, William Elliott, Andrew Fitzsimons, Jun Hanzawa, Marie and Seamus Heaney, Kazuo Kawamura, Edna and Michael Longley, Anne McCartney, Medbh McGuckian, Paula Meehan, Maureen Murphy, Isamu Nakashizuka, Nuala Ní Dhomhnaill, Francis O'Hare, Paul Perry, Poetry Ireland, Mikiro Sasaki, Giuseppe Serpillo, Helen Vendler, Joseph Woods, and the Yeats Society (Sligo).

Contents

Introduction

Nobuaki Tochigi

On the evening of 19 December 2001 at a theatre in Tokyo, Mutsuo Takahashi's Kyogen play (a farce usually played together with Noh) entitled *The Nonagenarian's Hair-do* was brilliantly played. After the final curtain, Sensaku Shigeyama, a living national treasure who acted the lead role, reappeared on stage to sing a song. It was written by Takahashi in a traditional Japanese style to celebrate the birth of the crown prince's first daughter. Consequently, the whole house paid homage to Empress Michiko, the new grandmother, who was sitting there among the audience. The event exemplifies Takahashi as a traditionalist, who is able to feel at home with such long-established poetic forms as haiku and tanka, as well as theatrical forms such as Noh and Kyogen. Yet, this is but one side of his resourcefulness; he is first and foremost a free verse poet who lives a cosmopolitan life.

Since the publication of his first collection of poems *Mino My Bull* in 1959 when he was twenty two years old, he has written eight collections of haiku and tanka and more than twenty collections of free verse poems. He is exceptional among contemporary Japanese poets not only because he is prolific but also because he goes 'beyond the hedge'. For example, haiku or tanka poets seldom cross over the specialized confines of the traditional forms, and poets writing in free verse tend to think of those established forms as anachronistic and of their music as metronomic. However, Takahashi has been outstandingly resilient in adapting different forms, including irregular and experimental *vers libre* for his own voice. In addition, his explorations in the world of books and arts has resulted in more than a dozen books of essays with topics varying from Japanese and Western literature—old and new—to novels, theatre scripts, even a libretto.

Orpheus is Takahashi's favourite poet figure to whom he refers again and again in his writings as if to confirm his own vocation. He thinks that for an Orpheus of our time, no Underworld exists, and for this reason, he cannot be persecuted, mutilated or annihilated in order to attain a renewed life. Our Orpheus has no choice but to view this world as the Hades where he must search for his own Eurydice. The poems in the first section of *On Two Shores* reflect Orpheus-Takahashi's responses to contemporary Hades. They are haunted with suggestions of the end of the world, questioning *sotto voce*: 'Are you, too, already done for?'; 'does it really exist?'; and 'What if it's …/The corpse of our century?' The poems which cast an observing eye on the 'war and genocide' of Pol Pot's Khmer Rouge, 'Ebola' virus, the 'Sarin' terrorism in Tokyo, and the fall of the 'twin towers of Babel' recall some of the most atrocious events in recent memory. However, it is a relief to find that images of 'light' are scattered throughout some of these nightmarish poems and that we, the 'terrorised', might 'be reborn/and flow out of the shimmering leaves as light'.

The group of poems from 'Faith' to 'In Ireland, I' is the fruit of Takahashi's visit to Ireland in the summer of 1999. He and the Japanese poet Mikiro Sasaki toured around Kerry, Sligo and Donegal, giving poetry readings in Dublin and Belfast. They were greeted with the hospitality of Nuala Ní Dhomhnaill, Cathal Ó Searcaigh, Theo Dorgan, Peter Sirr and Paula Meehan, among others; and their readings were joined not only by those poets but also by Michael Longley and Ciaran Carson. As the poems 'Beyond The Hedge' and 'Changing Places' imply respectively, the poet's experience of the place was so spiritually momentous that he left his heart in that other island and '… became the railway station out in the bogland,/and the station me, returning to my homeland'. The weeks spent in Ireland were decisive for Takahashi in regaining his faith in poetry. His Eurydice appears in different shapes in the poems: as the great book which was '*handmade by this country's writers and artists*', the stick which is 'growing bigger and bigger, as we all can see', and the well which 'everyone should have'.

Takahashi's excited imagination culminates in a small piece of hope, 'The Process'. The poem, written immediately after a poetry reading in the Ulster Arts Club, Belfast, does not celebrate the reading directly. Instead, it commemorates going 'up to the bar afterwards/to laugh and drink pint after pint of Guinness' as if to say that life as 'a process' is more important than poetry because faith in poetry is rooted in life itself. The poem ends with a toast to the city and the world 'going through a process'. An actual reading of the poem, 'The Process', with an English translation took place during Takahashi's second reading tour of Ireland in the summer of 2002, and a wonderful surprise happened—the Mayor of Belfast chanced to be among the audience of the reading in Gortahork, Donegal, to enjoy the poems.

Some works included towards the end of the present volume suggest Takahashi's state of mind after he came home from Ireland: 'On Two Shores' tells of 'the nightwalker' who awakes into reinvigorated meditations on here and there; 'Mistletoe' can be read as an adoration to his 'still verdant' mistletoe-muse. Surviving the anxieties of the turn of the century, the poet's soul is now given a renewed faith. This whole process for Takahashi might be conjectured from the titles of the collections from which the poems included here were taken and translated: *This World or the Man of Boxes* (1998), *Beyond the Hedge* (2000), *A Period of Recovery* (2001) and *Taking a Stick* (2002). 'The man of boxes' refers to the American artist, Joseph Cornell who made boxes or, according to Takahashi, 'the frames of wells/through which we can take a glimpse and be swallowed into the true world/where shadows had gone'. And a 'stick' here is an offering for the tomb of Shinobu Orikuchi, the great Japanese scholar/poet whom Takahashi admires so much. Takahashi says 'poetry grants us a forum where we are allowed to have a dialogue with people who died a thousand years ago'. Therefore, 'we may connect ourselves to different ages by quoting the words of the dead... and to do so links us not just to the past but to the future'. In this context, 'the dead help the living write'.

With a revivified faith in his own heritage, Takahashi ventured to compile the works he had written in various traditional Japanese forms into a single volume, *Following the Old Ways* (2001). The opening poem, a ritual Shinto prayer, was composed soon after his visit to Ireland in 1999 and significantly entitled 'A Tribute to the

Personal Helicon in My Backyard', which fulfilled his wish to clean his own well—a wish that was made in Donegal where he wrote 'Going to the Well'. So, it is encouraging to witness our Orpheus still on his pilgrimage with a spiritual companion whom he came across on his way to Santiago in the last poem of this volume, 'Dog Meets Man'. The pilgrim reminds me of the memorable ending of Jorge Luis Borges's celebrated short story, 'The Immortal', in which the narrator travels through different times: 'Words, words, words taken out of place and mutilated, words from other men—those were the alms left him by the hours and the centuries'.

——

A few words about the translators. Mitsuko Ohno is a Yeatsian scholar who has lectured frequently for the summer school in Sligo, and is a translator of Nuala Ní Dhomhnaill's poetry into Japanese. She also organized Takahashi's two tours in Ireland. Without Ohno's keen interpretation skills on each day of the tour, the poet's in-depth and intuitive understanding of Irish people and their culture could not have been fostered. Her translations, as well, of the poems for the reading tours were indispensable for the Irish audience. Frank Sewell is not only the author of academic books such as *Modern Irish Poetry: A New Alhambra*, but also a poet and translator whose view of translations as 'cover versions' is now taken almost as a norm by younger poets such as Gearóid Mac Lochlainn. Ohno and Sewell have long known each other, and Sewell's meeting with Takahashi, during the former's lecture tour of Japan in 2000, accelerated the pace of this joint project. The result is extremely truthful to the Japanese texts; the translations are amazingly rich and readable in English, as is shown in the phrasing, for example, of 'In Ireland, I' and 'Trilogy for Nuala Ní Dhomhnaill'. I must assure the reader that, in such poems, the allusions to Irish writers, including Muldoon and Yeats, are deftly begotten without at all abusing the original text.

二つの岸辺

高橋睦郎

Morning

One morning, you open your front door, and find
the world has ended.
Now, what are you going to do?
What can you do?
There's no inky-fresh smell of newspaper in the letterbox.
No milk bottles wet with dew on the doorstep.
Hold on a minute! There *is* no doorstep or letterbox.
The whole landscape which, until last night, consisted
of lines, colours and tangible things,
has vanished and left the world a complete blank.
To record what has happened,
you turn around and go back to your desk
but the writing pad you left open,
your pens and steaming mug of tea
aren't there anymore. It's all a complete blank.
You stand stock still before the missing door,
neither coming in nor going out.
Are you now a pillar of salt, standing there in your slippers?
Are you, too, already done for?
To say you are done for means
that you were destined to be done for,
the world bound to end,
the door's days numbered,
and that morning and evening
were not to be.

Terrified

One day the world we are in will end.
What a terrifying thought!
And since there will be an ending,
there must also have been a beginning.
And before the beginning, the world
must not even have existed at all.
What a really terrifying thought!
We are now living in a world
which previously did not exist
and soon won't. What a terrifying thought!
This world of ours is meaningless
and in this meaningless world
our lives are meaningless, too.
What a terrifying thought!
Terror is all we have to go on.
What a terrifying thought!
And the end of this terror will be
the same as before the terror struck.
What a truly terrifying thought!
So, please, let the terror spread and grow
until this whole meaningless world
is terrorised. And don't stop.

Courier

Recorded delivery!
A letter for you by special post!
One bright sunny morning, there's a knock at your front door,
and your doorbell, wet with dew, rings.
Who is it but the shining messenger always sent out
from the end of the world to the here and now?
For the future is an unavoidable conclusion
and the present always re-inventing itself.
I, the present, never sleep.
I, the door, am knocked and knocked.
I, the doorbell, am pressed over and over.
.worromot morf margelet A
.retal setunim evif morf emac tI
Under a halo of morning light, a courier-bike
arrives backwards without a sound.
The end of the world must be as bright,
blinding us in a single glare.

The Letter

I am writing a letter
addressed to you.
But
as I write,
you who will read the letter
don't exist yet;
and when you read the letter,
I who wrote it
won't exist anymore.
A letter suspended
between someone who doesn't exist yet
and someone who doesn't exist anymore –
does it really exist?

*

I am reading a letter
written by you who don't exist anymore,
and addressed to me who didn't exist yet.
Your handwriting wraps me up
in rosy happiness
or
plunges me in violet despair.
You who wrote the letter
are a light-source that ceased with the letter.
And I, reading the letter today,
am an eye that didn't exist back then.
The essence of a letter between
a non-existent light-source
and a non-existent eye
is light transmitted through darkness

from one non-existent sphere
to another –
but does it really exist?

*

He will read your letter.
He who didn't exist before,
and doesn't now,
but who belongs instead to a far-off time.
And as he reads the letter
from you who don't exist anymore but did,
the letter you wrote to me who didn't exist then but do now,
he will catch a reflection of rosy happiness
or
be eclipsed by violet despair.
Light emitted
from someone who doesn't exist
to someone who didn't yet,
and viewed by someone else again who doesn't yet exist,
that is to say, light emitted from nothing to nothing,
refracted and forwarded to yet another nothing,
the nothingness that the light beams across –
does any of it really exist?

Reading a Letter

I've brought the chair out into the garden,
the garden full of forget-me-nots,
to read a letter.
And as I read, I slip into a doze.
Who wrote the letter, and when?
Who and when have been forgotten.
Why did the letter have to be written
yesterday, and by you?
Who's reading, and when,
have been forgotten, too.
Why now? And why am I
the one to read it?
Only the letter stays open in the sunlight.
The garden slips into a doze,
the letter into a doze and
oblivion.

The Olive Tree

for Dani Karavan

There's not a lot we know about the olive tree.
While thousands of rippling leaves shimmer in the sun,
the roots reach down into the dark depths of the earth,
or so we think.
Rows of beard-like roots stretch out to embrace
layers of dead generations from down the centuries,
mixing and merging with their memory, joys and griefs,
or so we think.
The distilled matter seeping out of there
and sucked in by the slender tips of roots
to climb rough paths in the tree-trunk
and flow out lavishly as light,
is a mystery to us.
All we can do is sidle up to the tree
and sit down to rest, read, wait for someone,
talk or, sometimes, make sketches.
One of these days, death will pay us a visit,
and we'll join the serried ranks of the dead.
Siphoned-in by slender roots, we'll be reborn
and flow out of the shimmering leaves as light.
That much we know.

Fall

Instead of seeing the meteor-stream from Leo,
I slept through the sharp decline into the new century.
My friends climbed a windy hill to watch,
others took to the stillness of the sea.
And though the meteors did not rain down, as predicted,
did they reveal even a flash of the next century's skin?
Deep behind my closed eyelids, I'm sure I saw a light
with a tail behind it, diving down to the horizon
of darkest sleep. What was the light I saw?
The cold earth I sleep on? Or was it myself
sweating blood at closing my eyes forever?

Eyes

Spring, and down the hill from my veranda,
a garden just beginning to bud
is rocked by a stormy wind.
Past the garden, on the motorway
rising high up into the sky,
a stream of container lorries
carries something I cannot see
to somewhere I do not know.
What if it's a frozen corpse
lying there in the box-shaped darkness?
The corpse of our century?
Or of the world itself?
Perhaps the world has died before us,
and the dead world,
watched by its survivors,
is decaying bit by bit
like the carcass of a beauty,
showing the way of all flesh
before too long.
I wish I had eyes to see through dark,
an optical system free and independent
of flesh that rots upon the stroke of death
so that, when the world and all of us perish,
and time runs on or out,
my spying apparatus would float
in the dark mid-air,
blithely as the moon.

Everlasting Bread
for Emily Dickinson

The poems you wrote and left for us
have many faces and charms
but right now I want to see,
hidden away in the house somewhere,
the bread you baked every day.
But should I say *bread* or *breads* –
which is it?
Breads, perhaps, because you baked them
day-in, day-out. Or just *bread*,
if it always looked the same.
Bread or breads, it or they –
what did the bread/s look like?

In one of your most striking poems,
'Because I could not stop for Death',
you and your gallant death sit
side by side in a horse and trap,
slowly trotting towards 'a house
that seemed a swelling of the ground'
– that old familiar shape and shade.
First, it would look the same as always
but each caked surface must've been unique.
Unless we knead and make anew
each morning, our 'house in Eternity'
also loses its freshness and softness.

The Cedar

Grandma said, *The day you were born,*
I planted a cedar tree on the mountain.
Today, it's yours. You can build a cabin
to live in or sell it for money — it's up to you.
There's no more milk for you to suck
from my wrinkled leather dugs.
Aah, the cedar! As old as I am.
I'll take an axe and chop down that sturdy tree,
hollow the trunk into a fresh-made coffin.
I'll push grandma into it alive, nail down the lid
and, on a moonless night, launch the cedar out on a silent sea,
marrying for all eternity my grandma, old as the earth,
to the cedar, young as the sky.
And so I'll bid farewell to poor grandma.
Only she, the cedar, and I will know,
and my crime will become my cabin.
There will I live like a sad, spineless snail,
carrying my cabin around with me until the day I die.

Fifteen-Year-Old

Pure and innocent. Innocent and pure.
In the post-war poverty of fifty years ago, was I really so innocent
at fifteen, in my school uniform and starched, stand-up collar?
Yes, I was. So full of innocence. And of pure evil.
Hating people with such violence. Dreaming of killing them.
But I did not kill. For, when I went out to murder,
the trees and waters before me kept shifting and changing
until my hatred soon dissolved into the scenery.
Today, the whole townscape is artificially fixed and set,
leaving nothing to dilute the bloodlust of fifteen-year-olds.
Casting no shadow, the fifteen-year-old of fifty years ago
smiles and says, *I wish the waters and trees hadn't been so giving.*
Otherwise, I could've been pure. And a murderer. A murderer. And pure.

The Round Table

One long-drawn-out October morning,
the wooden table was delivered from a distant past.
Hand-made in England 200 years ago and more,
the solid round table is big enough for six.
And though I'm well past my prime, and single,
I will spend the rest of my days like one long afternoon,
here at the table, breaking bread and spilling crumbs,
brooding over the latest draft of a poem.
Sometimes, sipping peppermint tea with a young guest,
I will talk about the end of the world.
Whenever the world finally ends,
what dark hole in the universe
will this table and chairs be sucked into?
The new books and old letters that we've read here,
our child-like laughter — where will they land?
Will my soul, long departed from my body,
sit around here like a memory, and never leave?
Rambling on, with my two elbows on the wooden table,
I won't notice the night fall.

To the Terrorist, Ezra Pound

As year one ends in a new millennium of turmoil,
I sit by the fire, flicking through pages of a book
of photographs from your final years in exile:
standing straight with the help of a cane, you gaze
deep into a maze of water in wintertime; or,
with lovers dozing in the summer background,
you look windswept under a giant, lush-leafed tree;
or, celebrating your 81st, you stand expressionless,
surrounded by raised glasses. In one photograph,
piles of paper and a portrait of you, black-bearded
and in your prime, are stacked carelessly on a shelf.
Back then, you were a power to reckon with, a terrorist
of the word. On national radio in a country at war
with yours, you rounded upon your homeland
for reducing itself to a stock exchange. Arrested,
imprisoned, finally you were banned from the U.S.
The lines on your forehead grew deep as furrows
on the face of the earth. In a voice as hoarse
as the wind blowing over the frozen marshes,
I can almost hear you spitting out the words:
My life was a total waste. Poetry. Politics.
Everything—a total waste....
But if *that* was a waste, then Creation itself,
especially the birth of humankind and what followed,
is a bigger waste or, worse, a typo that can't be fixed.
Three decades after you left us devastated by your loss,
the arrogant stock exchange of your country
swelled up thousands and thousands of times over,
sucked two iron birds into its twin towers of Babel,
and imploded. Perhaps, the world itself imploded.

It hasn't hit home yet and, when it does, we'll all be gone:
you, the album, and the photo of you strolling along
the water's edge. But your words of warning
will keep on sounding a reminder no-one will hear
across the galactic marshes where stars burn out.

Tale of a Grass Spirit (Perhaps)

'To keep you is no gain, to destroy you is no loss'
—slogan of Pol Pot's Khmer Rouge, circa 1976

Cities are evil. They consist of brothels,
foreign exchanges and schools, you declared
and cleared from every door and alley
the residents of Phnom Penh.

You purged each building and window in fire.
When people turned the other cheek,
you slapped and stamped them to the ground.
Under a searing sky, you marched

two million barefoot to the end of the road,
made them kneel in a scorched field
at sunset and dig the stony soil
with their nails until they bled.

When they could move no more, you smashed
their necks and spines with rifle-butts,
and left their bodies in the grass,
to bear the insult of the night dew.

You were never wrong.
Your eyes, clear as water, prove it.
But don't stop there. Don't
rest your hands that torched the cities.

Go on, and burn down the villages.
Your wrinkled brows lashed the merchants,
let them lash the farmers, too,
and wipe out every human being

down to the youngest until you destroy
the root of all evil, all
humankind in the darkness that remains.
And when there's no-one on earth but you,

with a serene smile on your face,
you can raise a stone to bludgeon
the root of life between your legs.
Your body will rot where it's smashed,

and grass, piercing the wound, will dance
in the wind. Grass and trees
will be the order of the day.
For what drove you to genocide,

to making the font of life an abyss,
was not you yourself, perhaps,
but something that got into you,
a grass spirit, a will-o'-the-wisp.

Ebola

Our origins are ancient,
as ancient as our source is invisible.
Huddled closely together, with nothing dividing us,
our voice lowered to a whisper,
we flow under the skin of time
on a dark riverbed.

As always, we were on our way somewhere else
when you, on your way, rested in the cool shade of a tree
and, play-acting, held a baby monkey in your arms.
Play-acting, it bit you
and, from that bite, we flowed into your body,
flooding every blood vessel,
searing every cell,
breaking the skin of every organ.

And so we continue quietly on our way,
disposing of you as we pass through
with your scent and voice imprinted on our memory.
What drives us is neither joy nor sorrow
but, if you must give it a name,
love that never ends.

Carriers

On 20th March 1995, members of the Aum Shinrikyo cult entered
Tokyo Underground and released sarin, a deadly nerve agent.

Sarin. The word, *Sarin*, sounds so beautiful,
breezes in as fresh as the sound of *sayasaya*,
has the same cool ring as *rinrin*,
though the thing itself is a gross enigma.

Sarin, the source of that fresh, cool sound
was carried with closed eyes and silent reverence,
carried overnight, at full speed on the motorway,
to the north and Tokyo underground at sunrise.

The carriers – were they a few disciples of one blind leader
or the twelve million of us who live in these islands?
Will our *fin-de-siècle* be remembered for the hand-carrying,
and carrying out, of a light two-syllable poison?

No, for even now in a new century, we carry toxin
from heel to toe, toe to heel, carry and pass it on.
Sometimes we stop and put our heads together,
our tongues go through the ritual talks of resolution.

In the end, the meaning of the disyllabic matter
is identical in meaning to the dissyllable for
us: mankind. And for that, there is no answer
but to carry on, century to century, until it's over.

Faith

for Theo Dorgan

Day one, with the map in our minds still blank,
we are brought to a hill-top in the middle of town.
The poetry centre is upstairs in a castle watch-tower
where a neighbour ruled this land for 800 years.
Inside, young people work at computer screens
while 8 vertical windows give 8 views of the city.
Listening to impassioned words of faith in poetry,
I look up at the solid beams and bare rafters.
The sky, outside the windows, is overcast.
Will the world still exist in 800 years?
Who will be in charge? If everybody,
both the rulers and the ruled were dead,
and poetry ran the neo-natural order,
I wouldn't be surprised. It sounds strange
but I miss the world where no-one will live.
To miss the future is a contradiction in terms
but there's no other way to express this feeling.
Is it because I'm looking through the eyes
of the dead in 800 years' time?
This is The Great Book of Ireland,
handmade by our country's writers and artists....
You put on gloves to show us the priceless book.
And I, too, put my hands, that may have perished
8 years from now, into soft glove-shaped darkness.
Struck dumb with emotion, I turn page after page
that poets' hands (some now dust) have filled
with their deep faith in poetry living on.

Trilogy for Nuala Ní Dhomhnaill

1. In the Parlour

After laughing and drinking all night,
we each retire to our separate rooms.
One by one, the bedroom lights

go out until the only light that comes
into the hall is from the parlour.
There, in the hearth, a turf fire flames,

awaiting the return of any sleepless visitor.
All lovers in the myths of this place,
are wild and wilful as its nature:

a woman signals her husband is away
by pouring milk out into the river.
Caught with her lover, she turns and slays

her husband whose servant, to avenge his master,
leaps off a cliff, holding the mistress.
Her lover wanders, unhappily ever after,

on a guilt-ridden journey that never ends.
Over and over, the banked-up fire
keeps blaring out these myths and legends

through the wide-eyed window in the parlour
to the bay dreaming further tales
of master, servant, wife and lover.

2. From a Sandbank

From a sandbank, a whisper of snipes call out,
Come away, come away.
But step closer, and they all fly off,
leaving nothing on the sand
but a crazy pattern
of three-pronged footprints.

From the pages of an ancient manuscript,
lovers on vellum call out,
Come away, come away.
But look closer, and nobody's there.
Only the perfect past flowing into the plain future,
the future plunging into the past.

3. Crossing the Stream

I'm going to take off my shoes,
tie the laces round my index finger
and, dangling a shoe from each hand,
walk barefoot on the beach.
Over sand and trickles into the bay,
I'm going to cross two shallow streams,
and walk out to the burial ground,
hidden in tall, sun-dried grass.
Legend is, there lies a coffin
and, in the coffin, a sleeping woman,
carried here from a desert land,
oceans and centuries away.
I want to meet this saint or legend.
Village women come and dance
to praise the sleeping saint, counting
the days of her endless repose
on sand slipping between their fingers.
I want to meet those ghost dancers.
Papyrus plants all over the bay,
the tombstone in the marram grass
risen into a giant pyramid...
In broad daylight, I'll meet this vision.

The Poet's Stick

for Nuala Ní Dhomhnaill

To lean on, over thorny paths and sharp stones.
To point at the far crests of waves in the wind and sun.
That's all I ever knew a stick was good for.
But handed down from wise old hand to young,
this stick makes the holder's hand grow before our eyes
while the stick itself grows from within.

Embarrassed, you want to hand the stick to someone else
but we would rather you held onto it longer,
walking through fields of heather and wild strawberries
because, tight in the palm of your hand,
the stick suckles your blood and body-heat,
growing bigger and bigger, for all to see.

Three Poems in Memory of W. B. Yeats

Cast a cold eye
On life, on death.
Horseman, pass by!
—from 'Under Ben Bulben'

1. The Tower (Ballylee)

By a dark river there's a stone tower ringed by trees.
Inside the stone tower, a winding staircase of stone.
The man inside the stone tower walks the stone staircase,
peering out a stone window at the world below.
Outside the stone window, an age-old battle rages on:
friends killed by friends, brothers by brothers.
And when the tide of blood begins to ebb,
the man inside the stone tower leaves the stone door,
never to return. Inside, in a stone-faced room,
stands a hearth of stone. There a turf fire
burns silently on and on in memory of the man
who lived in the stone tower, and never returns.

2. The Autograph Tree (Coole Park)

Here stands a mighty beech, two armfuls in girth,
with names and initials carved into the bark –
reminders of those who stayed at the house
and strolled the garden. Several of the names
remained on close terms, others did not.
Two began as friends but, later, parted.
The lady of the house welcomed them all
with open arms, taking them under her wing
like the branches spreading down around the tree.
Entering their fragile shade this autumn day,

we have fun deciphering the scrawls and initials.
The lady and owners of the autographs have gone.
Soon we also will leave the tree and go
far away, never to return. So far away
that all the signatures etched into the bark
will seem like figments of our imagination.

3. The Bridge (Sligo)

From the four stone arches of a bridge,
shadowy water gushes and flows.
We watch it from the riverbank
as he did, a hundred years ago.

One day, he left the riverbank
and toured many towns and gardens,
ending his days in one last garden
in a far-away town. His coffin

crossed the bridge when he returned
to enter the garden of the dead,
beside the highroad. How many towns
and how many gardens will I visit

when I have left the riverbank
and crossed the bridge? What kind of bridge
and town will my remains be borne
across? What kind of man will watch?

Beyond the Hedge

The rain was pouring on Carrowmore
that cold September morning.
On every hill of the ancient site,
rows and rows of cairns,
some big, some small,
stood in broken lines.
Deep in thought under his wide umbrella,
our guide suddenly pointed beyond the hedge:
See the swaying ring of trees
beside the stone wall on the hill?
People go in there to think,
and always come back in tears.
Why? No-one knows, but there's talk
of some mysterious power.
Pressed for time, we got into our car
and left the shadowy ring of trees behind,
unvisited. That night I dreamt
my heart was softly weeping there alone,
the trees swayed over my hotel bed,
and light poured down through the leaves,
speaking intimately to me in its own tongue.
The meaning sank into me like water
but now it is impossible to translate.

North

for Cathal Ó Searcaigh

Further up towards the North Pole, the road
rises. On either side, the grass is short
and houses back away from each other.
The window of our B&B looks onto the bog,
the shore and, in the distance, white waves.
After sunset, the evening turns cold and dark
as, one by one, doors open and locals
with fiddles, flutes, guitars and accordion,
head for the house with all the lights on.
They nod to each other and wait by the fire
until everyone is sitting comfortably.
At last they open their instrument cases
and, at a signal, strike up and play
until they run out of tunes. Their thoughts
entrusted to their strings and bows,
they drink tea, bow politely and leave.
But my soul that cannot entrust itself
to anything, slips through a gap in the door,
turns into the piebald waves, and howls
off-shore until the night-clouds burst.

Changing Places

Driving north across the bog, we saw
something strange, and stopped the car:
an abandoned rail stop with no destinations.
Once, great catches of herring passed through here.
You could almost snatch them with your bare hands
from carriages piled high with crates and crates
of fish bound for the market towns down south.
Later, the fish changed course to another shore
and new roads were built for trucks.
Carriages were hacked to pieces. Rails left to rot.
Now the station building and one platform
stand knee-deep in heather with no-one around.
I got out of the car, and saw not just a building,
but a life, a fate. Not a 'thing' or 'it'
but an 'I'. Myself, perhaps.
Was it *me* standing there looking at *it?*
Or me, perhaps, who was being looked at?
Me in the car, closing my eyes as we pulled away,
and the *station* that stayed behind to watch us leave?
I became the railway station out in the bogland,
and the station me, returning to my homeland.

Going to the Well
for Cathal Ó Searcaigh

'Everyone,' he said, 'should have their own well.'
Those words of wisdom, fresh as sun-dried hay,
hit home to us, as we crossed hill after hill

of bogland. Guided down to the bottom of a hill,
we found a well, and as the wooden lid was lifted,
a shallow body of turf-coloured water trembled.

It reminded me of an old abandoned well
in my own backyard far away;
long sealed-up, its water stained with oil.

When I go home, I should clean that well.
Or, first, find and clean the well in me.
The fallen leaves covering up my well

back home are nothing compared to the well
of apathy long stored-up and nursed in me.
Here the water, drawn fresh from the well

and stored in a clay kitchen pot, settled.
Sharp and clear as the blue patch of sky
peeking through a hole in the clouds, it thrilled

my tongue and throat. Everyone should have a well.

The Process

for Michael Longley and Ciaran Carson

Did we read our poems in the hall downstairs
just so we could go up to the bar afterwards
to laugh and drink pint after pint of Guinness?
And did the audience just play along,
waiting patiently for the reading to end
so we could all unwind up here with a drink?
To say so doesn't take away from poetry.
For if my poems serve as a step up
to a higher place, they'll have done their bit.
Come to think of it, the poems that we read
have stayed behind in the blacked-out hall below.
Gathered gloomily around a chair, they
are listening closely to the laughter from above.
Right now, it's quiet here. The place at peace.
Belfast, the world, is going through a process.
I raise my glass: *here is to the process!*

Foxes

for Ms Kazuko Yokoo, former ambassador to Ireland

A fox wanders in and out of this garden, she said.
So, just where the hall light petered out on the lawn,
the lady-of-the-house scattered morsels of meat
from an iron pot, and stepped into the shade.
We followed, like it was the thing to do.
There was a hedge, some shrubs
and, in the distance, a dark pond glistened.
To talk with a tree, you have to get right in close to it.
And maybe it's the same with a fox,
if you think about it from a fox's point of view.
There and then, led on by the lady ambassador, we became foxes.
Every morning the feathers of one small bird are scattered,
she said, *so the eaglet in the branch can grow.*
The fox, too, has to survive,
and the human.
Then and there, we felt hungry, took our leave
and headed straight for McDonalds where the burgers,
as we tore into them, smelled faintly of fox.
But the scent of fox, in the garden
and as we attacked our burgers,
came from our own teeth
and tongues.

Visiting Kilmainham Gaol

1.

Five steps from door to back wall,
three from left to right. High up
on the back wall, a window
for light, and close to the wall
a wooden bed, table and
chair. Seems an ideal living
space to us but hell itself
to a resident. The door
opens whenever we want.
Knowing so reassures us,
frees us, though all we can do
for now is look at the sky
through the bright window, and wait
for the door to be opened.

2.

It resembles an hotel,
this grand hall of iron stairways,
the neat rows of doors with small
windows facing each other
on every floor. But no-one
goes in or out these doors, just
meal-trays through the small windows.
Residents have no contact
with each other, and an iron
net divides the floors. Inside,
hope for freedom or, rather,
fear of death resides. Day by
day, fear turns into resolve,
and resolve, one morning, turns
itself sharply into fact.

3.

At the far end of the yard,
penned-in between high stone walls,
residents are ordered to
stand in line. One, unable
to walk, is tied to a chair.
The number of residents
corresponds exactly to
the number of attendants.
The latter level their guns
respectfully, the former
slowly bow to the ground. Death
stands up in their stead each time,
climbs freely over the walls,
roaming streets and villages
like bad news to inflame and
inspire their comrades-in-arms.

4.

Inside the high stone walls, a
boat is trapped, a sailing boat
arrested as a rebel.
Being a boat is a crime
in this fettered, stony place.
Catching the wind in its sails,
a boat goes where it wants, when
it wants, beyond the limits
of tides and currents until
it sails into the dark ends
of the galaxy. Freedom
like that should not be allowed,
such longing locked up in irons.

5.

Thrown out the open iron door,
we walk on cobbles outside
the jail, and cross a stone bridge
to catch a double-decker
into the weekend rush hour.
Soon we're laughing and chatting,
dunking soda bread into
soup, and raising frothy pints
of stout. There, in the distance,
stands the hill and, on the hill,
the jail like an old fortress.
Visit the jail once by chance,
and you are bound to return.

Potatoes

Potatoes are delicious.
And dug fresh from the soil
they are even more delicious.
Put your spade into the ground,
and potatoes bob up, one
by one. You would think the soil
could never run out of spuds,
but it wasn't always so.
Winters came when year on year,
digging produced only stones
and holes in the ground. Without
spuds, people starved, shrivelled up
and died. Their shrunken bodies
were thrown like seed-potato
into more holes in the ground.
There they decayed and dissolved
until darkness, cold and time
turned them into potatoes.
Outside, each potato has
a pained expression. Inside,
tiny blood vessels run through
a tangled network of veins.
If you bake a potato,
the aroma is rich. Rich
with burning blood and despair.
Slit an X into the crown,
add butter, devour with joy,
and you're devouring in your maw
the hunger and death of thousands,
of hundreds of thousands
who fell on the frozen soil.

In Ireland, I

Every night in Ireland, I
got up in the wee small hours and tidied my luggage,
put on my trousers, a pullover, and stepped out into the dark.
The air that struck my cheeks, the sand and soil under my feet,
all of it was wide-awake. I sensed it in every pore.
The trees were the kind whose juices flow to the tip of every twig.
And the birds, every one of them had a soul of its own.
The sea was alive as the first time I saw it,
and the sky as the day it was born.
It was clear, clear beyond a shadow of a doubt
that one day this beautiful world would end.
Just as each and every moment I've felt alive was too rich,
and each and every moment could be the last,
in Ireland, I was always getting ready to move on.

On Two Shores

The nightwalker steps quickly along the beach
from the east to the west side of the strand
and turns back east. At right angles to his steps,
the sea from another shore far across the world,
closes its white teeth softly in.
Two weeks ago on that other shore,
he sensed, somewhere beyond the wind,
the shore which, now he knows, is here.
Tonight's walker then was standing still
but waves closed in the same as now.
At the furthest tip of land, the sea and shore,
as far as the eye could see, kept changing places.

The Cliff

for Ryuichi Tamura

The second millennium began with a one
and stopped at nothing.
How will the end of the second millennium look,
viewed from the start of the third? For example,
will it be like a sea-cliff soaring up to the sky?
I remember seeing, a long time ago,
a lonely graveyard at the edge of the red continent.
To get there, I crossed the sea by night-boat
and rode an early morning bus that shook me awake.
Beyond the graveyard was a cliff.
I crawled my way to the brink, and saw
on the ragged rocks far below
the white rim of the blue sea
snap at the body of a fallen calf
swollen with salt water,
its bared yellow teeth and pink ribs protruding.

That was the view from the cliff-top.
But if you were to turn around
and look up at the cliff from below,
you wouldn't know what was up there.
All you'd see is the blue, unfathomable sky,
and the little boat you stand on
rocked by waves rising higher and higher.

Mistletoe

In a dream one February afternoon,
what looked like mistletoe appeared to me
and told me to write a poem about it.
Lodged between earth and sky, mistletoe
sprouts into the air from a tree-trunk.
Even in winter, when the parent tree withers,
the mistletoe's leaves are still verdant.
So, donning a sweater, coat, scarf
and gloves, I went out to see the mistletoe.
The frosty evening sky was cloudless
as I stood on the jagged edge of a sea-cliff,
staring at some mistletoe in a tree-top.
Its green berries in the setting sun
glowed with a strange passion and intensity
but after sunset, they were just black spheres
in the blue wind, pregnant (it seemed) with seeds
of fire or lightning. Their image imprinted
on my mind, I returned home.
And this is my poem. My mistletoe poem.
I wrote it under the lamp on my desk
in a room filling up with darkness.

Echo

for Takao Ono

Morning Angelus, evening Angelus,
on the tongues of thousands of bells
echoing between heaven and earth,
in paintings of the life of Christ
on old church and cathedral walls
where Lorenzo, Giovanni, and Alessandro,
amid crowds who heard His sermons
or saw His robe stripped from Him,
aim hard stares back at the viewer.
The faces and eyes of these liars
and real-life hypocrites soon fade
in time like their memory
but are restored over the years
by brush-strokes, drawing them out
from walls and murals, bringing the colour
out of their *quattrocento* clothes
into the bright *novecento*
where today's colourful crowds
see out the second millennium
as Gianfranco, Guido, Pierpaolo....
Don't blame them for the lack of faith
in their modern faces and eyes.
Before these towns and cities were born,
God was always with them, the crowds:
Morning Angelus, evening Angelus,
on the tongues of thousands of bells
echoing between heaven and earth.
God said always, says now and forever:

Blessed art thou,
the unfaithful.
I am
because thou art
unfaithful to Me.

Nectar

at the ruins of Antigone's shrine

A bald-headed grocer now occupies
the residence of the mythic princess,
she who was given in marriage to Hades
for burying her kinsmen with honour.
The black-veiled bride will still be known
when the short-sleeved grocer is forgotten.

The fruit and veg on his dusty stands
are known by their earthly names:
figs, pomegranates, carrots, garlic.
Their scent, stronger than flowers,
attracts insects whose golden wings
were fashioned in another life
spent crawling in the earth's labyrinth.

A traveller myself from darkness
to darkness, I stand before the grocer
and pick up one or two of his fruits
to refresh myself and brighten up.
From seeds, they came through darkness,
and now are full. Full of nectar.

Dog Meets Man

Does a man's soul come in the shape of a man,
and a dog's in the shape of a dog?
If so, your doggy soul
was glad to see my human soul
blown down the dusty highway
like a scallop shell
one summer long ago.
I threw you a piece of bread
left over from the hotel breakfast.
You ate a little, dug a hole to hide the rest,
and caught up with me,
tagging along for miles on end.
As sun was setting on the open road, I began to worry,
and threw a stone at you, aiming to miss.
You looked at me doubtfully,
tears swelling in your eyes at once.
I tried not to look back.
Since then I've wandered many a highway.
I wonder, have you?
A dog's life, they say,
is a fifth the life of a human.
So, if your days in this world are done,
and mine go on just a little longer,
your doggy soul
and my human one
may soon be walking side by side
like two old friends.
Ahead of us the road runs on into the sunset and beyond.
A moonlit road, bright as the livelong day.

お前は疑わしそうに私を見た
その目にみるみる膨らむ涙を
私はつとめて振り返らなかった
その後　私は多くの街道を歩いたが
お前はどうしたろう
ヒトの五分の一というイヌの
お前のこの世の生は終わったとしても
私の生はもうすこしつづくとしても
お前のイヌ型の魂と
私のヒト型の魂とは
親しく寄り添って歩いている
たぶん　それはあの夕日の道のつづき
昼のように明るい月の道

49

イヌ　人に会う　Dog Meets Man

ヒトの魂はヒト型
イヌの魂はイヌ型をしているのだろうか
そうだとしたら
あの遠い夏の
帆立貝に導かれた乾いた街道で
お前のイヌ型の魂は
私のヒト型の魂を見て喜んだのだ
ホテルの朝の食べのこしのパンを拋ると
少しだけ食べて　残りを土を掘って匿し
はるか先を行く私に追いつき
何処までも　何処までも　ついて来た
夕日の道で　さすがに気になり
わざと外して　石を投げた

闇から闇への旅の途中の者として
この世の八百屋の前に立つ
できるだけ軽く清い者になるために
果物の一つ二つを取り挙げる
それらも種子という閉ざされた闇を
経て来た　蜜に満てるものだ

蜜　Nectar

神話の王女の住居の領分を
いま禿頭の八百屋が占めている
父親と兄弟とを弔った褒美に
冥府との婚礼を贈られた花嫁に
半袖シャツの八百屋の名は忘れられるが
喪服の花嫁の名は伝承される
埃っぽい台の上の野菜や果物なら
イチジクとかザクロとか
ニンジンとかニンニクとか
この世の名で呼ぶことができる
花よりも強い匂いに昆虫が来る
その黄金の翅は　土の迷宮の
匍匐の生活の中で用意される

第二の千年紀末の原色の雑沓に紛れ込んだ

ジャン＝フランコやグイドやピエル＝パオロ

現代の目たち　顔たちの　砂漠のような背神を言うな

それらの都会　それらの町町の生まれる以前から

神はいつも彼等　群集とともにあった

朝のアンジェラス　夕のアンジェラス

天と地とに谺しあう千の　万の鐘の舌の中

神はいつものたもうた　のたもう　のたもうだろう

さいわいなるかな　汝らの背神

汝ら我に背くが故にわれあればなり

谺　Echo

小野隆生の肖像たちに

朝（あした）のアンジェラス　夕（ゆうべ）のアンジェラス

天と地とに谺（こだま）しあう千の　万の鐘の舌の中

古い町町の寺院の壁の　色あざやかなキリスト一代記

説教するキリストや衣（ころも）を剥（は）がれるキリストを取り囲む群集

の中から　するどくこちらを見る

ロレンツォやジョバンニやアレッサンドロ

当時実在の　偽善の　不信の目たち　顔たちは

記憶のように　時とともに薄れ　消えかかり

思い出したように差し向けられる鉛筆の先に　修復され

修復の絵筆に学習され　壁画の外　寺院の外へ

衣装を千四百年代（クワトロ・チェント）から千九百年代（ノベ・チェント）に脱ぎ換え　着換えて

日没ののちは　青い風の中の
黒い球となってしまったヤドリギたち
裡に稲妻の火の種を宿すとも見える
私はそれを目に焼きつけて帰って来た
そして　これがヤドリギの詩だ
もうすっかり暗くなった机の
電気スタンドを点けて　書いた

ヤドリギの詩　Mistletoe

二月の午後のうたたねの夢に
ヤドリギらしい植物が現れて
自分のことを詩にせよ　と言う
ヤドリギは天と地とのあいだ
大木の幹から宙にむかって萌える芽
親木が枯れた冬もみずみずと緑の葉
セータと上着の首に襟巻
両手に手袋を嵌めて見に行った
澄み凍って雲一つない暮れがたの
海を眼下に　切り立った崖の上
見上げる梢の　いくつものヤドリギ
沈もうとする太陽が　緑の球たちを
はげしく　あやしく　輝かした

56

だが　それは崖の上から覗き込む海

こんどは逆に　下の海面から振り仰ぐ崖

崖の上に何があるにせよ　それは見えず

見えるのは　底知れず深い空の青のみ

おまけに　見上げる者の立つ小舟は

昂りやまない大波に　揉まれっぱなし

57

美しい崖　The Cliff

田村隆一に

1で始まった二番目の千年紀は　0で終わる
三番目の千年紀の始まりの地点から見る
二千年紀の終わりの眺めは　どんなだろう
それは　たとえば海面から天へするどく切り立った崖
私は思い出す　遠い光の中のひとつの風景
赤い大陸のどんづまりの　棄てられた墓地
夜の海を船で渡り　早朝のバスに揺られて行った
墓地の行き止まりは崖で　腹這ってこわごわ覗くと
青い海の白い縁が噛む　ごつごつした岩の上
足を辷らした犢の死体が　塩水を吸って膨らみ
剥き出しの黄ばんだ歯と桃色の肋をあらわにして

58

二つの岸辺　On Two Shores

夜歩く人は早足で波打ちぎわを
砂浜の東の端から西の端まで歩いて
折り返し　東の端まで戻って来る
彼の歩みと直角に　重い夜の海が
白い歯を見せて　音もなく寄せている
とおい　とおい　向こう側の岸辺から
二週間前　その岸辺に立っていたのだ
その時　吹きつける風の中で感じていた
見えない向こう側は　ここだったのだ
今の夜歩く人は　昼に立つ人だった
波だけが同じにしらしらと寄せていた
見はるかす固い干潟の先の先
絶えず位置を変える波打ちぎわまで

つねに自分のこの世の旅を整理していた

アイルランドで

アイルランドで私は　　　In Ireland, I

アイルランドで私は　　　毎晩
夜なかに起き出しては　旅の荷を整理した
ズボンを穿き　セータを被り　まだ暗い外に出た
頬にぶつかる空気も　　靴底が踏む砂つっちも
すべてが目覚めているのを　切実に感受した
そこでは樹は小枝の先まで血液の通う樹
鳥たちは一羽一羽　別の魂を持つ鳥たち
海がはじめて見るようにあたらしいから
空が生まれたばかりのようにみずみずしいから
この美しい世界がいつかは終わることが
疑いを容れる余地なく　確かに信じられた
生きていると感じる一瞬一瞬が痛いほど甘美だから
一瞬一瞬のいつ終わってもいいように

61

ジャガイモは一箇一箇苦しい表情をし内側には細かい血管が網の目のように入り組んで走っている

ジャガイモを焼くと血と絶望の焼けるこうばしい匂いが立つ

その匂いにナイフで十字を入れバターを落としてほくほくとむさぼる

昨日の凍てついた土の上の数十万人の飢えと死とを歯を鳴らしてむさぼる

ジャガイモ　Potatoes

アイルランドの旅では毎日ジャガイモを食べた

ジャガイモはうまい

土から掘ったばかりのジャガイモはとりわけうまい

土にシャベルを立てるとジャガイモは後から後から出て来る

土は無尽蔵にジャガイモを産みつづけるように見えるがいつもそうだったわけではない

掘っても掘っても石ころしか出て来ず掘った穴ばかりがあっちにもこっちにも残る冬が何年も何年もつづいた

ジャガイモが食えなくて飢えて痩せさらばえ死んで種イモのように干からびた人人は残った穴に投げ込まれた

死体は穴の中で腐り蕩けつめたい闇の時間の堆積の下でジャガイモになった

63

開かれた鉄の扉から吐き出されて
私たちは塀の外の石畳を歩く
石橋を渡って　二階建のバスに乗り
週末の街の雑沓の直中に下車する
泡を冠ったギネスのグラスを挙げ
スープにソーダパンを毟り込む
談笑する私たちの遠景に丘
丘には牢獄が城のように聳える
縁あってひとたび牢獄を訪ねた者は
いつの日か　必ず牢獄に戻るだろう

4

高い石塀の中に船が囚われている
叛徒の一味として打捕された帆船
鎖された石の空間にとっては
船であることがすでに罪なのだ
帆という帆にいっぱい風を孕んで
行きたい時　行きたい先に向かう船
ついには潮流の埒を超えて
銀河の果ての闇へも走り去ろう
そんな自由が許されてはならない
憧れは鎖で繋がれねばならない

65

3

高い石塀に鎖された庭の行止り
住人は並んで立つことを命ぜられる
中には立てず　椅子に縛りつけられた者も
住人と給仕人の人数は正確に同数
給仕人は恭恭しく銃を構え
住人たちはゆっくりと崩おれる
代わって立ちあがるのは死
死は自由に塀を乗り越える
街や村を噂となって徘徊し
仲間たちを激昂させ　鼓舞する

2

この吹抜けの大空間はさながらホテル

各階両側にドアと小窓が整然と並ぶ

しかし　ドアから出入りする者はなく

小窓から食事の盆が出入りするだけ

内側の人が互いに連絡しあうこともない

しかも　上階と下階には隔ての金網

ドアの内にいるのは自由への希望

というよりはむしろ　死への不安

不安は日日　確信へと成長する

確信はある朝　突然事実に変身する

67

キルメイナム監獄を訪ねて Visiting Kilmainham Goal

1

扉から突当りまで歩いて五歩
左の壁から右の壁まで三歩
突当りの壁高く　明り取り窓
壁ぎわに粗末な木のベッド　机　椅子
私たちにとっては理想の生活空間だが
住人にとっては地獄そのもの
扉は開けたい時にはいつでも開く
と思うことの自由と落ちつき
明かり取りの空を見上げるだけ
扉を開けることがほとんどないにしても

68

おお　一匹のキツネを生かすためにも
一人のニンゲンを生かすためにも
私たちは急に空腹を覚えて　辞去した
私たちの跳び込んだマクドナルドのハンバーガーは
歯を当てると　かすかにキツネが匂った
いや　あの庭と同じキツネの匂いのもとは
ハンバーガーに跳びかかった私たちの歯であり
舌だった

狐の庭　Foxes

駐アイルランド大使横尾和子さんに

「この庭にはキツネが出ますの」
広間の光の届くぎりぎりの芝の上に
女主人は鉄鍋から肉のかけらを撒いた
それから　闇の領分に入って行った
私たちは当然のようにそれに従った
草むらがあり　灌木の繁みがあった
繁みの向こう　暗く光る水があった
「樹と話すには　樹の真下に行きませんと」
たぶんそれはキツネの位置　キツネの目線
女主人を先頭に　私たちはキツネだった
「あの枝に棲むタカの雛一羽が育つためには
毎朝　一羽分の小鳥の羽毛が散らばりますの」

ここはいまのところ静か　じつに静かだ
この市も　世界も　何かへの過程にある
ともかくも　過程に乾杯！

過程　　**The Process**

マイケル・ロングリーに　キアラン・カーソンに

ついさっきまで階下のホールで朗読したのは
そのあと　笑いながら階段を上って　このバーで
ギネスの泡立つグラスを重ねるためではなかったか
聴衆だって　ここでくつろいで飲むために
階下の椅子で我慢して　耳を傾けていたのでは？
そう言ったからとて　詩を卑下したことにはなるまい
何処かいっそう高いところへのステップになれるなら
私の詩も　以って瞑すべしではなかろうか
そういえば　朗読した詩をそのまんま
電灯の消えた階下に置き忘れて来たような
忘れて来た詩たちが　椅子の上にかたまって
階上の笑い声に耳を澄ましているような

72

さらに夥しい内側の怠惰の堆積を思った

甕に貯め置かれた泥炭の井戸の上澄みは

蟠る曇り空の裂け目から覗く空のように

するどく冴えて　舌とのどに喜ばしかった

井戸を捜す　　Going to the Well

人はみな自分の井戸を持つべきだ

それは　　泥炭の丘また丘を旅していて

教えられた枯草の匂う知恵の言葉

導かれた井戸は　丘のふもとの窪み

立てかけられた木の蓋を取ると

ふるえている泥炭いろの浅い水量_{かさ}

私は　　遠いわが裏庭の忘れられた古井戸

蓋をしたままの油の浮いた水を思った

帰ったら　あの井戸を凌_{さら}えなければ

それよりも　　私自身の内側の井戸を

凌えるよりも前に　まず捜さなければ

私は　わが家の井戸蓋を埋める落葉より

74

それは三人称のそれではなくて
一人称の私であるかもしれなかった
私はそこに立って見ている私ではなく
見られているそれであるかもしれなかった
走り出した車の上で目をつぶったのは確かに私か
車の後ろに残って見送ったのは間違いなく駅か
私は駅になって　　　泥炭の野に残った
駅は私になって　　　私の国へ帰って来た

75

交換　Changing Places

北の海に向かう途中の泥炭の野で
私たちは不思議なものを見て　車を停めた
行き先を失って　棄て去られた鉄道駅
かつては素手で獲れるほど大漁つづきの
ニシンを箱に詰め　箱を重ね　積み込んで
南のにぎやかな町町まで運び届けた
その後　魚の群は目指す岸辺を変え
トラックの道が別のところに開通して
貨車はばらされ　線路は錆るに委せた
人一人見えなくなったヒースの野に
駅舎と一つきりの歩廊だけが残された
私は車から下り立ち　そこに見た
ひとつの建物である以上にひとつの運命

頷きあって　知る限りの曲を奏であう
語れない思いを絃と弓とに託して語り
熱い茶を飲み　辞儀深く帰って行く
何ものにも自分を託せない孤立した魂は
内から固く鎖した戸の隙間を脱け出し
泥炭地の沖の波がしらとなって　叫びつづける
重い夜の雲が裂け落ちるまで

北へ　North

カハル・オー・シャーキーに

北の地軸に近づくほど
道は上り坂　両側の草の丈は低く
草の中の家家は寄り添わない
思いつめたような窓から見えるのは
荒れた泥炭地につづく荒れた干潟
干潟のはるかに　白い波が立ち上がる
寒い夕焼が終わり　日が暮れると
あの戸口　この戸口から　楽器を持った人人
灯った一つの家を目指して　集まってくる
人人は火の前で親密な挨拶を交わし
つつましやかに自分の椅子を確保する
徐ろにケースから楽器を取り出し

その夜の宿の夢の底で知った
ベッドに木立がかぶさっていた
葉むらから光がそそいでいた
光は光の言葉で親しく語りかけた
私はそれを水がしみるように理解したが
いま　私たちの言葉に反訳はできない

柵のむこう　　Beyond the Hedge

大小　何十という石積み墓が
不規則につづく遺跡の丘　また丘
丘には　九月の午前の冷たい雨
大きな傘を掲げた考える人は
突然　柵のむこうを指し示した
あちらの丘の石積みのそば
揺れている木立が見えますか
あの木蔭に行って瞑想した人人は
かならず涙を流しながら帰ってくる
理由は知らず　不思議な力があるらしい
予定が詰まっていたので　車に乗りこみ
私たちは　その木蔭には行かなかった
行かなかったが　心だけは残して来た
残して来た心が静かに涙を流すのを

多くの都市と多くの庭をめぐり
遠い都市の遠い庭で　　生を終えた
柩は橋を渡って　この都市に戻り
街道沿いの死者の庭に葬られた
私はこの川岸を去って　　橋を渡り
幾つの都市　幾つの庭をめぐるだろう
亡骸は　　どんな都市のどんな橋を渡るだろう
どんな人が　　川岸から見ているだろう

八方に拡がり　枝垂れた枝枝が　幹を包んでいる

女主人は去り　名前の主もみんな退場

九月の　すこし疲れの見える日蔭に入り

あれは誰　これは誰　と興じる私たちも

間もなく　樹を後ろに　遠く去って帰らない

木肌の上の名前がすべて幻だった　と

思わずに!はいられない距離まで

Ⅲ　橋　スライゴー

石づくりの橋の四つのアーチから

奔り流れる黒い水を　川岸から見る

百年前　その人が見ていたように

その人はある日　川岸を去り

石の塔の人は　石の戸口を出て帰らない
石の部屋の中には　大きな石の暖炉
石の暖炉の中には　記憶の泥炭の火
再びは帰ってこない石の塔の人のため
聞こえない音を立てて　燃えつづける

Ⅱ　樹　ゴルウェイ・クール荘園

ここに二抱えものブナの大樹があり
木肌に　名前や頭文字が彫りつけられている
この屋敷に招かれ　庭に遊んだ人人の記念(かたみ)だ
名前どうしは仲が良かったり　悪かったり
中には　初め仲良く　後で悪くなった二人も
彼らのすべてを　女主人が微笑で包んだように

83

イエイツを思い出す三つの詩

Three Poems in Memory of W. B. Yeats

鞍の上つめたき目投げ行きすぎよ

わが生ける日も死してののちも

W・B・Y

I　塔　バリリー

木立の中　黒い川のほとりに石の塔

石の塔の内側には　回る石の階段

石の塔の人は　石の階段を上り下り

石の窓から　塔の外の下界を見まわす

石の窓の外の下界では　長い闘い

友が友を　兄弟が兄弟を殺しあう

闘いの波が海の潮のように引いた後

84

杖が　あなたの血と熱とを貪婪に吸収して
成長しているのが　はっきり見えるからだ

杖持つ人に　The Poet's Stick

シェイマス・ヒーニーから詩人の杖を
渡されたヌーラ・ニー・ゴーノルに

茨の茂る瓦礫のぬかるみ道を衝いて歩く
晴れて風のある沖の波がしらを指し示す
そのほかに　杖の用途があるとは知らなかった
年長の知恵深い手から年若い賢い手に　手渡す
手渡されたことで　手は目に見えて成長し
杖じしんまた　内側から成長する
あなたは面映ゆそうに　手渡された杖を
早く別の誰かに手渡したい　と言うが
私たちとしては　もうしばらく手に握って
ヒースや野いちごの野を迷ってもらいたい
あなたのてのひらと密着していることで

86

入江いちめんがパピルスに覆われ

枯草の中の墓碑がピラミッドに成長する

まっぴるまの夢に会いに行こう

両手にぶら下げて
砂浜を素足で歩いて行こう
砂の上の入江に注ぐ流れを
浅い二つの流れを渉って
夏枯れの丈草の中の
すたれた墓地へ行こう
遠い砂漠の国から
幾億の波が手渡しで
何百年かけて運んだという柩
柩の中に仰臥して眠るという
聖女の伝説に会いに行こう
聖女の眠りの気の遠くなる日数を
指の股から零れる砂粒で数え讃え
一日じゅう踊りつづけるという
村の女たちの幻に会いに行こう

だけど　砂を踏んで近づくと
一羽残らず　飛び立ってしまう
砂の上には　三本ずつの足跡が
入れ乱れて　残っているだけ
まるで　古い写本の筆跡のように
羊皮紙の恋人たちは呼んでいる
コーイ　コーイ
だけど　近づくと誰もいなくて
清冽な過去が凡庸な未来へ注ぎ込むだけ
過去にむかって未来が打ち寄せるだけ

Ⅲ　流れを渡って

靴を脱いで
靴紐を指に搦め

89

密会を見つけた夫を　逆に殺してしまう

夫の従者は殺された主人の復讐のため

女主人を抱擁して　高い崖から落ちる

女の恋人は自らいのちを消耗するため

終わることのない自責の旅に出る

それら　荒削りの挿話の一部始終を

火は　問わず語りにしゃべりつづける

客間の大きな硝子窓の外　枯原の向こう

入江は　別の愛の神話の夢を見ている

Ⅱ　砂洲に立って

砂洲に降りたつイソシギの群が呼ぶ

コーイ　コーイ

90

ヌーラ・ニー・ゴーノルに献げる三つの詩
Trilogy for Nuala Ní Dhomhnaill

I　客間で

夜っぴて飲み　笑い声を挙げていた連中も
みんな　それぞれの寝室に引き取った
寝室の窓の灯りがすべて消えた後
客間だけが灯って　廊下に開いている
壁の暖炉には　泥炭があかあかと燃え
眠れなくて起きて来る客を待っている
この土地の神話の恋人たちは　男も女も
この土地の自然のようにまっ直(す)ぐ(ぐ)で　激しい
女は夫の留守を小川に乳を搾って報らせ

91

かつて支配した者　支配された者　人間はすべて絶え

恢復した自然を詩が支配しているというのなら　わかる

人間がいないという世界が　妙になつかしい

未来がなつかしいというのは矛盾のようだが

やはり　なつかしいとしか言いようがない

八百年後の死者の目で見ているからだろうか

「これがこの国の詩人たちの手造りの一冊だけの本」

あなたはその貴重な書物を　手袋付きで見せてくれる

八年後には消滅しているかもしれない両手を

手袋型の柔かい闇にゆっくり辷り込ませ

詩人たちの手が思い思いに書きしるした

人間がいなくなっても存在する詩への熱い信頼を

説明できない感動とともに　めくって行く

その手のいくつかは朽ちて　すでに無い

信頼　Faith

テオ・ドーガンに

頭の中の市の地図もまだ白紙の最初の朝
連れて行かれたのは街の中心の丘の上
訪ねる詩の家は　この国を八百年支配した
隣国の城塞の　望楼の石段の上り止まり
縦長の窓は八方に　窓からは市の八方が見え
窓の中では　若い人たちがコンピュータと向かいあう
部屋の中央で詩への熱い信頼の言葉を聞きながら
天井の剥き出しの岩乗な梁や椽を見上げたり
窓の外の曇りがちの空の表情を眺めたり
八百年後　外の世界はまだあるのだろうか
その時　世界を支配しているのは何者だろうか

93

あしゆびを次ぎ　くびすを次いで　はこびつづけながら
ときに立ちどまり　額をあつめ　舌をあつめて
解明の儀式を　やくたいもなくくりかえす
この物質の二音節の意味は　ついには
私たちを指す二音節の意味に同じだから
解明はとこしえになされることがない
とこしえに解明されることがないから　私たちは
はこびつづけ　はこびつづけるほかはない
世紀から世紀へ　世の終わりまで

運ぶ人　Carriers

サリンというひびきは単純に美しい
不可解なおそろしい実体をはなれて
さやさやとさわやかで　りんりんとすずしい
そのさわやかですずしいひびきの実体を
まぶたをおろして　うやうやしくはこぶ
夜の国道を北に向けて　全速力ではこび
暁の階段を地下に向って　無言ではこぶ
はこぶのは　盲目の人に導かれた何人かではなく
この島島に住む一億二千万の私たち全体ではなかったか
私たちの重くるしい世紀末は　この軽やかな二音節の
実体をはこびはこんだことで記憶されるか
いや　新しい世紀に入ってもなお　私たちは
はこびつづけ　はこびつづけているのではないか

あなたという旅籠を壊し　通過して
あるいは　あなたの声と匂いとを
ひとりひとりの記憶に刷り込んで
私たちの沈黙の旅はつづく
それは喜びでも悲しみでもない
あえていうなら
休むことのない愛

旅する血　　Ebola

私たちの来歴は古い
源が見えないほど古い
私たちは隙間がないほどひしと抱きあい
声をひそめて　　時の皮膚の下
暗い川床を流れつづけて来た
私たちはいつでもどこでも旅の途中
あなたが旅の途中の涼しい木陰で
戯れに抱いた仔猿の戯れの咬み傷から
あなたの中にひそかに流れ込んだ私たち
あなたの血管という血管で荒れ狂い
細胞という細胞を発熱させ
臓器という臓器の皮膚を破って
洪水のようにあふれ出した私たち

97

さみどりの優しい草の精霊

かもしれない

だが　きみはとどまってはなるまい

都市を焼いた手をゆるめず　村落を焼き

商人を打った眉根で　農民を打ち

悪の根源である人間を　赤子の果てまで

闇のうちに根絶やしにしなければならない

すべての人間を滅ぼした末に残るただひとり

きみ自身を　きみの股間の生命の根を

石で潰した時　きみの唇には

美しい微笑がうかんでいるだろう

きみの肉体は潰されたそこから腐り

開いた穴を草が貫き　風にそよぐだろう

繁茂する草と木の夜明けが訪れる

きみに宣言させ　人間という人間を滅ぼさせ

きみの生命の根を暗い穴に変えるのは

きみ自身ではなく　きみの肉体に寄生した

99

草霊譚　　　　　　　　　　　Tale of a Grass Spirit (perhaps)

都市は悪である　なぜなら都市は
売淫窟と両替所と学校とで出来ているから
そう宣言して　きみは戸口という戸口
路地という路地から　住人を追い立てた
建物という建物　窓という窓に浄めの火をかけ
振り返る頬を平手で打ち　土足で踏みつけた
天の火事の下　長い道のりを跣足で歩ませ
道の果て　日の暮れの焼畑に跪かせた
血になるまで　爪で石土を掘り返させた
動かなくなると　銃の尻で首の骨を砕いた
草むらに棄てて　夜露の凌辱に委せた
きみはけっして間違っていない
きみの水のように澄んだ目が証明している

100

しかし　あなたの警告の言葉は鳴りつづけるだろう

誰ひとり聞くことのない記憶の谺として

星たちの死に絶えた銀河という潟の上を

あなたは　吐き捨てるように言う
自分の人生は　大いなる無駄
詩歌も　運動も　すべてすべて無駄
しかし　無駄といえば　天地創造じたい
とりわけ人類誕生とその後の歴史こそ最大の無駄
無駄という以上に　取り返しのつかない誤植
あなたが大きな不在感を残して去って　三十年
何千倍にも　何万倍にも膨張しつづける
あなたの国の　ふん反りかえった証券取引所・
二つのバベルの塔が二つの鉄の鳥を吸い寄せて
自爆したのは　おそらく地球それじたい
私たちがその事実に気づくには　時間がかかる
気がついた時　私たちはいないだろう
私たちはいなくなり　地球はなくなり
もちろん　あなたの写真集も　写真集の中の
水のほとりをさまようあなたもいなくなり

自爆

102

テロリストE・Pに　　　To the Terrorist, Ezra Pound

動乱の新千年紀第一年　年の暮の燃える火の前
あなたの流謫の晩年を写した写真集をめくる
杖をつき背筋を伸ばして　　冬の水の迷路を見つめるあなた
夏の輝く大樹の下　　昼寝の恋人たちを背景に立つ蓬髪のあなた
八十一歳の誕生日の祝杯たちに囲まれた　　無表情のあなた
写真の一枚には　　無造作に書類を重ねた棚があって
壮年の鬚濃いあなたの肖像画の複製が　やはり無造作に
当時の力満ち満ちたあなたは　　言葉のテロリスト
あなたの国の敵国のラジオから　くりかえし
証券取引所と堕したあなたの国を糾弾しつづけた
あなたは国によって囚えられ　　幽閉され　　追放されて
額には地球の表面と同じほど深い皺の束
凍る潟を渡る風のようなしわがれた声で

103

若い笑い声は　何処を落ちて行くだろう
肉体を離れて久しい私の魂の記憶は
まだ消えもせず　漂っているだろうか
木のテーブルに両の肘と腕を預けて
とりとめもなく　思いを遊ばせる
いつか来ている　濃い夕暮の中で

木のテーブルで　　The Round Table

十月の　水のように流れやまない朝
不確かな過去から　木のテーブルが届いた
二百年以上も昔の英国で作られたという
六人は優に囲める　岩乗な丸テーブル
私は折返し点を過ぎて　一人暮らしだが
残る人生の　長すぎる午後のような時間
このテーブルで　パンを毟り零したり
詩の下書きを推敲したりして　過ごそう
時には若い客と二人　薄荷の茶を喫み
地球の終わりについて　語りあおう
地球が終わる時　このテーブルは椅子ごと
宇宙の闇の何処へ　吸いこまれるだろう
ここで読んだ新しい本や　古い手紙や

105

十五歳　Fifteen-Year-Old

純粋　純粋　五十年前の貧しい世界で
十五歳の詰襟の僕は　純粋だったか
そう　透きとおるほど純粋に悪だった
人をはげしく憎み　殺すことを真剣に夢みた
殺さなかったのは　殺意を持って外に出た時
目の前の木や水が絶えず動き　絶えず形を変えて
憎しみの形をいつか風景の中に溶かしてくれたから
いま　風景はことごとく整形されて動かず
十五歳の殺意を薄めてくれるものは　何もない
五十年前の十五歳は影なく笑いながら言う
木も水も優しくなんかしてくれなければよかった
そうしたら　僕は純粋な殺人者になれたのに

106

大空ほど若い杉との永遠の婚姻
生涯不幸だった祖母への私の賭け
杉と祖母と私しか知らない犯罪こそが
私の小屋　私はその小屋に住み
その小屋を死ぬまで持ち歩こうと思う
暗鬱で臆病なカタツムリのように

杉　　　The Cedar

祖母は言った　「お前が生まれた日

山に杉を植えた　今日お前に与えるから

お前の住む小屋を建てるなり

売ってお金に替えるなりするがいい

私の乳房はしわしわの皮ぶくろ

お前に吸わせる乳はもう出ない」

おお　杉は私と同いどし　私は

鉞をふるって　抵抗する彼を切り倒し

刳りぬいて　匂いのいい棺を作ろうと思う

祖母を生きたまま押し込め　蓋を釘打ち

無月の音のない海に押し出そうと思う

それは大地ほど老いた祖母と

ゆっくりと駆け　ゆっくりと辿り着いた先

「地面が盛り上ったような家」その懐しい色と形

見たところ　いつも同じ顔をしているようだが

焼き上りの表情は微妙に異なっていたにちがいない

あなたのいう「永遠の生」の棲み家にしても

毎朝新たに捏ねなおし　作りなおさなければ

たちまち柔かさと馨わしさとを失ってしまうだろう

109

永遠のパン　**Everlasting Bread**

エミリ・ディキンソンに

あなたが書き残して　私たちが読むことのできる
たくさんの顔を持つ魅力的な詩たちよりも
屋敷深く私たちから身を隠して　毎日焼いたという
同じ質朴な顔をしたあなたのパンが見たい
だが　一つのパン？　それとも　たくさんのパン？
どっちで呼べばいいのか　私たちは迷ってしまう
毎日焼かれたたという意味では　たくさんのパン
同じ顔をしている点では　ただ一つのパン
それ　または それらは　どんな顔をしていたか
あなたの魅力的な詩の中でも　とりわけ魅力的な詩で
「死のために止まれなかったので」とあなたが語る
あなたが紳士的な死と並んで乗り込んだ馬車の

110

それは遠くない日　私たちの肉体の

辿るべき運命の先取り

闇の中に入りこめる目がほしい

突然死に　ゆっくりと腐っていく

肉体から　完全に独立した視機構

世界が滅び　私たちが滅んだあと

時間は存在するか　時間が滅んだあとも

闇の中空に月のように涼しく浮かんで

見つづける透明な穴

をあらかじめ

目　Eyes

坂の途中の縁側から見おろす
芽吹きの庭は　明るい嵐に揺すられ
庭のむこう　空高く架かる高速道路を
ひっきりなしに通るコンテナーは
知らない何処に　見えない何を運ぶか
走る箱型の闇に横たえられたものが
冷凍された死体だとしたら
私たちの世紀の死体　いや
世界そのものの死体
人類より先に　世界が死んだ
死にそびれた私たちが観察する
私たちより先に死んだ世界の
美女の死体のような刻刻の変質

112

降下するもの　Fall

獅子座流星群は　見なかった　新しい世紀への傾斜を　昏
昏と眠りつづけた
友人の何人かは　草の吹き立つ丘に登った　何人かは　押
し黙る海の沖へ漕ぎ出した　降るというほどではなかった
というその光は　来たるべき百年の皮膚なりと　照らし出
したか
私は　暗い眠りの地平線に尾を曳いて急降下する光を　目ま
な蓋深く確かに見た　その光の正体は　私の眠る冷えきっ
た地球だったか　赤い汁を噴いて瞑る私自身だったか

113

髭根の先に吸いこまれ　樹幹の路を通って
光としてそそぎ出される奥深い秘密を
私たちは知らない
ただ　その樹の傍らに行って　腰を下ろし
憩い　読み　待ち合わせて　語らい
ときにスケッチするだけだ
遠い日か近い日か　訪れる死を受け入れ
地の底の死者たちの堆積に加わる
髭根に吸い上げられ　葉のそよぎから
そそぎ出される光に転身する
それだけだ

114

オリーブの樹について　The Olive Tree

ダニ・カラヴァンに

オリーブの樹について
私たちの知るところは少い
その幾千の葉は　　真昼間の光の中に
こまやかにそよぎ　さざめいているが
その根の届いている大地の底の濃い闇を
私たちは知らない
根から伸びる無数の髭根の抱く
幾十代　幾百代の死者たちの堆積を
重なりあい　　溶けあい　一つになった
彼らの記憶を　　その悲しみと喜びを
私たちは知らない
それらから滲み出る純粋な物質が

115

手紙を読みながら　　　Reading a Letter

ワスレナグサの咲きみだれる庭に
椅子を持ち出して　手紙を読む
読みながら　うとうととまどろむ
その手紙を書いたのは　いつのたれか
書いた時と書いた人とは忘れられて
（書いた時が昨日で　書いた人があなた
でなければならない理由があろうか）
読む時と読む人も忘れられて
（読む時が今で　読む人がわたし
でなければ　なぜならないだろう）
ただ　光の中に手紙がひろげてある
庭はうとうととまどろんでいる
手紙もまどろんで　そして忘れられる

116

薔薇いろの幸福の反射を受ける
あるいは
菫いろの絶望の投影に翳る
存在しない者から
存在しなかった者に宛てられ
別の存在しなかった者が眺しむ光
無から無へ放射され
屈折して　さらに別の無へ
光の渡る深淵
それは存在するのか

存在しなかった目
のあいだにある手紙の本質は
存在しない天体から
存在しなかった天体へ
闇を超えて届けられる光
それは存在するのか

＊

手紙を読む
昨日存在せず
今日も存在しない
遠い明日の彼が
今日存在しない昨日のきみの
昨日存在しなかった今日のぼくへ
書いた手紙を読んで

＊

手紙を読む
きみが書いた手紙を読む
まだ存在しないぼくに宛てて
すでに存在しないきみが書いた
きみの筆跡が　　ぼくを
薔薇いろの幸福で包む
あるいは
菫いろの絶望に浸す
手紙を書いた昨日のきみは
書き終えると同時に存在を止めた光源
手紙を読む今日のぼくは
その時点では存在しなかった目
存在しない光源と

119

手紙　　The Letter

手紙を書く
きみに宛てて書く
だが
ぼくが書く時
手紙を読む明日のきみは
まだ存在しないし
きみが読む時
手紙を書いた今日のぼくは
すでに存在しない
まだ存在しない者と
すでに存在しない者
とのあいだの手紙
それは存在するのか

120

今朝も光をまとって
後向きに着く自転車
終末は目がつぶれるほど
明るいにちがいない

使者　Courier

「ゆーびーん」
「速達ですよーおお」
朝日を照り返す玄関の戸が叩かれる
朝露に冷たいベルが押される
それは　　世界の終わりから現在へ
絶えず発せられるまばゆい使者
終末という未来は動かない
絶えず動いて形がないのは現在
現在という　　つねに寝不足の私
私という戸はくりかえし叩かれ
私というベルはくりかえし押される

「チーこ書留のらや日田」
「ーすーこぬや熱ぬ五」

122

と同じだ　と考えることは　決定的に怖ろしい

お願いだ　この意味のない宇宙がいっぱいになるまで　怖

ろしさを成長させつづけ　増殖させつづけてくれ　やめな

いでくれ

123

恐怖する人　Terrified

私たちのいるこの宇宙がいつか消滅する　と考えることは
怖ろしい
宇宙に終わりがある以上　始まりがあったはずだ　始まり
以前には宇宙は存在しなかったはずだ　と考えることは
さらに怖ろしい
かつて無く　やがて無い宇宙に　いま私たちが生きている
と考えることは　怖ろしい
この宇宙に何の意味もなく　意味のない宇宙に　私たちの
生きていることに何の意味もない　と考えることは　怖ろ
しい
怖ろしいと感じることだけが　私たちの存在の実体だ　と
考えることは　怖ろしい
怖ろしさが終わることは　怖ろしさが始まらなかったこと

124

すべては何もない　まっ白
外に出ることも　内に戻ることもできず
消えた戸口の前に立ちつくして
きみは素足に下駄を穿った塩の柱？
きみもすでに終わっているか
終わっているというなら
きみはあらかじめ終わり
世界はあらかじめ終わっていた
戸口はあらかじめ消去されていた
朝もなく　ゆうべもなかった

125

朝　　Morning

朝　玄関の戸を開くと
世界は終わっている
きみはさしずめ用のなくなった身
さて　これからどうすればいい？
新聞受にインクの匂いの朝刊はない
牛乳箱に露を噴いた牛乳瓶はない
それ以前に　新聞受も牛乳箱もない
ゆうべまで線と色と質感とで出来ていた
風景が消え失せ　世界は白紙
事の顛末を記録するために
机に戻ろうと　くびすを返しても
広げた原稿用紙も　鉛筆も
湯気を立てていた紅茶も

二つの岸辺

高橋睦郎

ON TWO SHORES
New and Selected Poems

Mutsuo Takahashi

Translated from the Japanese by
Mitsuko Ohno & Frank Sewell

DATE D' ‾

2012

Printed in the United Kingdom
by Lightning Source UK Ltd.
115504UKS00001B/601-615

9 781904 556497